Let's Munch Lunch!

By Cameron Macintosh

Let's munch on lunch!

Nick's lunch is a hot pot.

Mum dips lots of things
in the pot for Nick.

Yang sips lunch in a mug.

Yang sips it
as it is too hot!

Tiff grills yams for lunch.

Tiff grills chops, too.

Yum!

Dad's lunch box is big!

He can munch on fish and pods.

pods

fish

Chad has dill in his lunch.

The dill is on Chad's eggs.

Chad's eggs look like a cat and a chick!

dill

eggs

Jill can munch a box of nuts with lunch.

Quin can not have nuts,
but he can munch
on this jam bun.

Such hot jam!

We sit on the dock for lunch.

I munch on fish and chips.

It's such fun to munch
my lunch!

CHECKING FOR MEANING

1. What does Nick have for lunch? *(Literal)*

2. Where does the dill go in Chad's lunch? *(Literal)*

3. Why do you think Quin can't have nuts? *(Inferential)*

EXTENDING VOCABULARY

munch	What does the word *munch* mean? What are other words that have a similar meaning? E.g. chew, chomp, gobble.
with	What is the last sound in this word? Make lists of words with the letters *th* at the start, in the middle and at the end. Share them with a partner.
dock	What is a *dock*? Is there more than one meaning? If you have a charging dock at home, what do you use it for? What do ships do at a dock?

MOVING BEYOND THE TEXT

1. What are healthy foods to have for lunch?

2. As well as healthy food to eat, what should you also have with lunch?

3. What foods are you able to buy for lunch at your school canteen?

4. What are some foods that people can be allergic to?

SPEED SOUNDS

sh	ch	th	th	ck	ng
		voiced	unvoiced		

PRACTICE WORDS

munch

lunch

Nick

Yang

things

fish

with

chick

Such

dock